Why the Corrida

Claire Callahan

Photographs

By

Michael Crouser

BleakHouse Publishing
NEC Box 67
New England College
Henniker, New Hampshire 03242
www.BleakHousePublishing.com

Robert Johnson – Editor & Publisher
Sonia Tabriz - Managing Editor
Liz Calka - Art Director

Shirin Karimi - Senior Creative Consultant
Erin George, Charles Huckelbury, Chris Miller, Susan Nagelsen,
& Saba Tabriz - Consulting Editors
Rachel Cupelo – Marketing Editor
Carla Mavaddat - Assistant Art Director & Curator

ISBN-13: 978-0-9837769-3-2

Printed in the United States of America

They say I did it.

They say I took it. Took a man's life. And one of their own at that. A man so close to them, like a brother, but still a perfect stranger to me - dead at my hands.

Or so they say.

Romero, breathless, swallows hard, fighting for air. He'd just finished a forced march from the basement of the jail to the basement of the courthouse, a place of justice with its own players and its own rituals. The most mortifying of these, the 'running of the felons', the unceremonious herding of the defendant in fast-moving lines from the jail transport vans past the media en route to the court house, a blur of bodies, buildings and cameras. At 2 metres and 100 kilos he towers over most men; but you wouldn't know it looking at him now. Head down, heaving for breath, perched precariously on a thin metal bench, Romero shrinks to half his real size. Dark purple rings frame his eyes as he scans the speckled cement floor, sticky from dirt and spit and other debris, things he doesn't want to imagine. His head hangs heavy, like a ball on a chain, supported by his hands, which enclose his face, hiding his pain. He shifts to the left. To the right. Trying to make the bench give-- if only just an inch underneath his weight, in a fruitless search for some small comfort. But the bench is unyielding; like the court, it seems, its position fixed. In no shape to call the officer back over for another plea, another chance, another explanation, Romero leans back against the wall. After all, their minds are already made up. Presumed innocent? Not likely. So he waits, bracing himself against the truth pushing its way to the forefront of his thoughts.

*They want someone to blame. And they say that someone…is **me**.*

Yes, he had run, and yes, he had struggled to free himself from the cop's grasp… or at least he thinks he did. His memory is hazy; he's not really sure what happened. It was mob scene. The game. The field. The drinking. The explosion of cheers…the applause. Then the riot—fists flailing, bodies flying. Really, what else could you call it but a riot? Everyone turned to instinct, each movement raw and uncertain once that fist hit his face out of nowhere. Excitement had morphed into anger, confusion…all of the action compiled in a matter of seconds. Whatever he did he did without thinking. He just reacted. Punch the cop? Strangle him? Maybe. He knew, if he was sure of anything at the time, he had to get out. He had to escape from that swelling mass of thrashing limbs. And surely, if he attacked the cop, it was in self-defense. He was in a fight for his life, wasn't he? What else could he have done? And he wasn't the only one. That much he knew, but they are making him doubt that now. This much he now knows for sure: He is the only one they caught, captured, and now brought here to the court, the arena at the heart of the law. In this adversarial system he enters as the enemy, the one who has to pay for the dead officer.

None of this mattered that night, of course, especially once the other cops leaped onto his back, forcing him to his knees. The scenes flash through his mind like a comic strip; the six policemen charging after him, their eyes blazing, the barrels of their guns glaring at his back until his labored breath finally gives out and he gives in, his frantic bid for freedom over.

Letting out a grunt, Romero tries to clear his throat of the lump threatening to rise and choke him. But it does not help. All he wants is to make them see him. Make them hear him. *I have to try again.* So he lifts his body from the bench and walks towards the iron bars that hold him. Wrapping his fingers around the bars, he looks around to get an idea of what he is up against. Suddenly, a door slams shut down the corridor - the sound reverberates against the metal bars in his hands. Shaking, he can hear the sound of his heartbeat.

They are not going to listen. They want to fight. And they want to win.

***

Beneath the scorching midday sun, the bull beats his hoof on the ground shooting puffs of dirt up from the dry earth. Slowly, he lowers his head, his dark eyes rolling upwards, peering through the wooden gate, unaware of what awaits him inside the arena. All he knows is that he wants in, to break free of his wooden pen and meet the cheering crowd hungry for the fight. On the other side of the gate is the torero- his match, his prey. The crowd roars in waves, crashing down into the center of the arena, honoring the bull's nemesis, who is dressed in a traditional beaded yellow jacket and red pants that gleam under the rays of sun. As the torero twirls his cape, the crowd is fixated on his sinewy frame. He flicks his cape to either side of the arena to pull the crowd in with his routine. Behind him the bull charges the wooden door, backing up a few paces to run forward and crash into it, shaking its hinges and scraping it with his horns. The crowd leans in, hanging off of the edges of their seats as the bull bursts through the door, charging into the ring.

The bull takes a lap around the ring, steadily approaching his prey. As he draws near, the torero pulls a scarlet cape along his side, causing the bull to stop short and size him up. As he sees the red cape rise, the bull snorts a defiant gust of hot air sensing that, if he takes this moment to charge, his horns will only puncture cloth, not flesh. The force of the gust raises the dirt into a hazy cloud around the two fighters, briefly suppressing their violent impulses. To run. To jump. To charge. *To kill.*

***

Romero senses that his new world is basic and primal, a court, still, but only one of last resort, featuring predator and prey, locked in a violent ritual. Standing behind the courtroom doors, Romero can already feel the heat of the jury's eyes searing into his skin. Preparing himself to assess the scene waiting for him, he fights down the hard rock of salvia forming in his throat and steps through the doors as they open to a full room, all eyes glued on him. He takes his seat as the warring prosecution and defense teams begin their routine, speeches spun from words seemingly without end, weaving connections among facts, or alleged facts, embracing witness after witness, dancing around each other. Their web of accusations hangs suspended in the closed world of the courtroom, and from it he dangles, caught in the intersecting strands of truth and lies.

They pull apart the evidence for the defendant in a verbal tug of war until he stands before them - no longer human - a mere pile of bones, the sinews dissolved in the acid of hostile words, lying there, on the floor, in a heap. At least this is how Romero feels – not just naked but barren, denuded. All he wants is a chance to get up and fight his accusers *mano a mano,* to take the bull by the horns, to be a real man, a man who can by his sheer force make the jury believe *his* words, not theirs, the words of the enemy, the words they seem to hang on with such conviction. Now a player in the ring, the court room is filled with mute and oddly menacing spectators, poised and waiting. Romero is forced to fight for his life; but not freely, like a man, never forgetting that he has to act according to their rules. Taking a moment to lean back in his seat, he watches his defense form a cloud of doubt around the prosecutor's accusations, hoping it will encircle the jurors and shield him from a certain sentence of death. At this moment, the prosecution swoops in, dispersing this temporal, protective fog, and with a flick of his wrist, somehow produces behind him a witness to the crime. The credibility of the witness is questionable, at best. Who can say, really, what really happened in the midst of the chaos of that night? Romero listens as this stranger spews lies, pointing at him, stabbing him with his words, drawing blood for all to see, giving the prosecutor his victory over what the state believes it rightfully owns – his life, claimed as payback for the life that was lost.

All the while the jury sits silently, peering at Romero through the mounting haze of fact and fiction, their culprit now slouched forward in his seat, mortally wounded. He follows the lines in the slick hardwood to avoid their gaze, wishing he could rise and shatter the deafening silence and make them believe the truth. His truth. The whole truth. So help him God.

***

The bull is restless from waiting, watching, and seeking cues from his rival to plot his next move. He moves with the torero, sliding to the right, turning to the left, hoping to synchronize their movements long enough to find his window of attack. Instantly, he springs off of his thick, muscular hind legs, launching himself at the matador's frame. The audience gasps; their collective breath hangs anxiously above the bull and his prey. *Could the beast really win?* The bull charges forward, his horns aimed directly at the matador's stomach. It would take but one jab into the soft belly of the matador for the bull to emerge victorious.

***

Finally, it is Romero's turn to approach the court, to somehow resurrect his case from the ashes left in the wake of the prosecutor's assault. He clenches his teeth, scraping them along his molars in an effort to steady himself, ready himself to launch his words.

7

Maybe now they will hear me. Thrashing about like a wild beast would not help him prove his case, but if words can wound, Romero must use them to make his attack. Self-defense, nothing more and nothing less. Just like before. *I must put up a fight.* The prosecuting attorney steps in front of him and lowers his brow into a furrowed line, pushing Romero with questions, parrying with him, pinning him down. Anxiously, Romero shoots a glance at the members of the jury, his eyes searching their faces for some sort of confirmation. *My peers? Can any of them understand? What are they thinking? Who will they believe? I see them... Do they see me?*

***

Suddenly, the crimson cape swooshes in front of the bull in place of the torero and the animal emerges on the other side of it, enraged, thrashing his head from

side to side in a desperate attempt to strike his tormentor in any way he can. Man and beast had exchanged spots like this for twenty minutes, feeling for each other's weaknesses. The torero thinks this next strike will end it all. And it is the beginning of the end. Outside of his limited peripheral vision, soaked in glossy sweat, the bull feels a sharp sting into his side, then another one deep into the muscle in the back of his neck, delivered by unseen spears wielded by the unseen man. Running forward, the dying animal stumbles to regain control of his head, angling his body to the right before colliding into the side of the rounded wall, revealing an open weakness on his left - his rage and quivering muscles a poor defense against the matador's cunning and relentless attack.

***

The jury moves silently, deliberately. They have rested, and they are ready, committed to playing their part just right. They file back into the courtroom, their shadows sliding along the wall, a man's fate in tow, a verdict poised on their lips. *Guilty.* No one cheers as the sentence—*Death*— pierces the silent room like a knife lodged into Romero's racing heart, cutting off all human reaction. The twelve phantom, now faceless, members of the jury shrink away from him, back against the wall. *It's over.* Romero hangs his head and slowly drags his feet towards the door, escorted arm-in-arm by a pair of guards—the capital sentence almost visible, like a dead weight on his sagging back.

Romero does not know it, but this is but his first in a series of deaths. More will follow outside of the courtroom, on death row, and finally, in the death house, each more final than the last.

***

The bull leans forward, his front legs stretched out just inches from the torero to meet "the third death". Three acts; three deaths; three men enter the arena to help the matador complete this, the final stage of the fight. It is now that the torero and his helpers must kill the bull for his crimes and sins, ultimately for being what he is, a wild animal in a tame world. Only then will man be cleansed of his own crimes and sins, his lust for the pure pleasure of fighting unto death, the bull's loss exemplifying the final conquest in man's battle with nature. The bull's heavy muscles slide him further into the ground as he bows his head to accept his fate. He cannot sustain another blow. This one will be his last. His eyes widen, and the last spear sinks in, tearing between his shoulder blades to puncture his heart.

The crowd's reaction is immediate. Elated cheers echo off of the edges of the arena as the spectators recapture their breath. *What spectacle!* The fans pour into the center of the ring, funneling through the gaps in the wall to reach their victor. Men, women and children cling to the gleaming torero, in awe of his strength and courage. They applaud his strategically brutal blows. For them, it is simple; man has once again defeated beast. The beast, yet again, is dragged out of the arena, lifeless and heavy, his fur glistening with tears of sweat and blood.

Romero is injected. Lethal chemicals course his veins. Paralyzed and expressionless, he lays still. Words fail him as he drifts into oblivion. This will be the final blow. He has waited for it for years, alone, the spectacle of his crime and punishment no longer of interest to the society that once thought of nothing else but sending him to his death for the death they claim he so carelessly caused. With only his executioner and official witnesses to watch, he takes his final breath. *Is this what they wanted? To dominate me? To annihilate me? To cleanse the world of my violence in place of their own?* His eyes flutter, and for a moment, everything is still. Romero is dead. And as the curtain closes the state emerges victorious. Man has once again defeated beast. But no one cheers. And no one takes a bow. If there is satisfaction, it is muted, discrete. This is not entertainment for all to see. Not suitable for public viewing. No, this is justice, solemn and sincere.

Or so they say.

Claire Callahan

Claire Callahan is an award winning honors scholar majoring in Law and Society at American University. Her record of achievement combines a thorough grounding in the humanities as well as law and justice, research interests that span national and international issues, fluency in French (for which she was awarded the *Upendra Lal Goswami Memorial Prize*), excellence in dance, and a passion for creative and academic writing. In June she published a law review article for the University of Washington Undergraduate Law Review entitled, *Adversarial Transplants in the Italian Criminal Justice System: The Amanda Knox Trial*. Callahan is also a Victor Hassine Memorial Scholar and has been selected as the editor-in-chief of the 2013 Tacenda Literary Magazine.

MICHAEL CROUSER is a prolific artist whose works include the award winning book, Los Toros (Twin Palms Publishers 2007). An exploration of the bullfighting around the world, *Los Toros* was awarded first prize in the category of Fine Art Book at the 2008 International Photography Awards. In January of 2012 Leica Gallery of New York exhibited "Michael Crouser: A Mid-Career Retrospective" which featured four distinct series from twenty-five years of his photography. Crouser's work can be found in the permanent collections of The Minneapolis Institute of Arts and the Museum of Fine Art, Houston.

Photographs by Michael Crouser were taken with permission from the book, *Los Toros* (Twin Palms Publishers 2007).

Why the Corrida is reprinted from the 2012 issue of
BleakHouse Review

Why the Corrida

A conversation between Robert Johnson, publisher, and Claire Callahan, author

Why the Corrida is your first short story, released to remarkable reviews. Few of us at BleakHouse Publishing, or any other press, for that matter, are compared to Hemingway at any time in our writing careers, let alone at the outset! So first, congratulations.

Thank you! I was shocked and delighted that my writing could be mentioned in the same breath as Hemingway's, because a great deal of my inspiration for the story came from his incomparable perspectives on the art of bullfighting. But in my mind, the reviews speak most highly to the support and nurturing that the *BleakHouse* publishing team gave me while I worked on the story. The comments and suggestions I received definitely transformed the story for the better.

What inspired you to write this story?

When I was sixteen, I spent a semester abroad in the southwest of France in a town called Dax, situated near the Spanish border. The area was rich with Basque traditions and Spanish influences, with mouthwatering paella on the menu and the corrida for choice entertainment. One afternoon during my stay, my host family took me to see the corrida at the arena in town, and it was there that I saw seven bulls killed in quick succession. For some reason, going into it, I did not realize that the bulls would actually be killed and dragged lifeless out of the arena, so when I saw the scene carried out several times that afternoon, I was stunned. Those images stuck with me and resurfaced as I learned more about crime and punishment, particularly the death penalty, three years later when I came to American University to study in the department of justice, law and society. I started to see more comparisons between the adversarial duel of the bullfight and the American adversarial justice system, which can be manipulated to the distinct disadvantage of the defendant in some cases, much as the bullfight is manipulated to the distinct disadvantage of the bull. And now that bullfighting has come under fire for being too violent, a barbaric vestige of the Spanish and Portugese traditions, I started to see the tragic similarities between those critiques of this blood sport and the United States' retention of the death penalty, a kind of legal blood sport.

You make those points quite artfully, and they stay with the reader. In a nutshell, what do you want your readers to take away from this story?

Admittedly, I am an abolitionist. I oppose the death penalty in any and all forms. My hope for the story is that readers will look at the death penalty from a different perspective, not as an act of proportionate punishment, but as a violent act that says something about the society that issues the sentence. To kill, the torero must display the same violence as the bull. So as a society, by killing the convicted, are we amplifying or wiping away the shared sin curse of violence? Romero is not entirely innocent, just as the bull is not innocent of acting violently when provoked, but when we execute, we act the same way, resorting to violence when we are provoked. We are hardly innocent, so we can no longer place all of the blame on the offender.

Which scene do you find most memorable?

The scene that sticks out most vividly in my mind is the bull's death – the third death, as it is referred to in bullfighting. I was morbidly fascinated by this ritualistic process as it was the last step it took for the torero to defeat the bull, paradoxically honoring it and conquering it at the same time. While writing, this scene was the clearest in my mind because of how it is choreographed to show that the torero uses his own controlled violence to stab the bull, using a swift series of movements to extinguish the bull's violent rage as quickly and precisely as possible.

What scene was the hardest to write?

As someone who is more comfortable with methodical, academic based writing, the entire creative writing exercise was out of my comfort zone. But what was hardest to convey was Romeo's crime scene. I could picture him fleeing, and I could see him in jail, but his actual offense was hard to depict. My goal was to liken him to the bull, as someone enraged, provoked, and overwhelmed by a series of events that quickly turned violent. This happens often in life, but it proved hard to capture. Because I had so much difficulty with the scene, it ended up being one of the last things I worked on. With suggestions from my editors, I was able to see the scene more clearly and really play with the psychological comparison between Romero and the bull.

I understand you are a dancer. What happens in the bull ring is a kind of dance, don't you think?

Yes, I would definitely agree with that. The bullfights I saw surprised me in how technical, yet at times elegant the movements were. To me, the bull, pawing his hoof on the ground, and the torero poised on his toes to lengthen the line of his arched back beside the bull reminded me of a bizarre *pas de deux* between the two fighters.

Pas de duex. A nice image. I can see that. What was your inspiration for the character, Romero?

Romero's character came from the second bull I saw killed at the corrida. I'm not sure whether I projected my own fears onto the bull, but I distinctly remember that bull acting with more caution than the first one. The fight was actually drawn out longer because of the bull's unwillingness to charge without abandon. It was clear that the crowd thought he fought well and respected him for it.

I was intrigued by that bull's mix of fire and hesitancy as it edged towards the torero, and I really related to it, instinctually and emotionally. That is why I wanted to weave the two storylines together, because to me, Romero and the bull are two forms of the same being. It is not just their shared instinct to use force and fight back, but their desperation and their ultimate hopeless acquiescence to the overwhelming power of their conquerors which unifies them. The unique element of Romero's character comes from the fact that Romero sees the imminent likelihood of his death, whereas the bull is so charged with rage that he does not stop to think or sense how he will ultimately leave the arena. And it was that foresight that I took from the second bull, because I think after the first bull was killed, the second bull felt something different entering into the arena. That intuition, if you will, prevented him from being wholly consumed by his violent impulses.

9 780983 776932